A Picture Book of

ANNE FRANK

DAVID A. ADLER

—Illustrated by—

KAREN RITZ

M

PAN MACMILLAN CHILDREN'S BOOKS

Anne Frank was born on June 12, 1929 in Frankfurt am Main, Germany. Her parents were Otto and Edith Frank. Anne had an older sister, Margot.

Anne's father was a businessman and had been a German army officer during the First World War. His family had lived in Frankfurt for hundreds of years.

Family portrait, c. 1900

Otto Frank, 1916

Anne was born during very difficult times. Millions of Germans were out of work. As people became more troubled, they listened to the hate-filled speeches of Adolf Hitler, the Nazi party leader. Hitler blamed Germany's problems on various groups of innocent people, but mostly on the Jews.

Anne, age 3

In January 1933, following an election, Adolf Hitler became chancellor of Germany. Jews lost their jobs. Their stores were boycotted. Books written by Jews were burned.

The Franks were Jewish and felt they had to leave their home and country. They moved to Amsterdam, Holland, where they thought they would be safe.

Anne's first years in Amsterdam were peaceful. At the Montessori School, her class was asked to write plays. Anne was full of story ideas. When the plays were put on, Anne was given the best parts because she was lively and outgoing. Anne dreamed of becoming a writer or a movie star.

Anne and her friend, Sanne

Anne at Montessori school, 1935

Anne (in dark dress) on her tenth birthday

Anne at Montessori school, 1942

But the hatred the Franks had escaped in Germany followed them. In 1939 the Second World War began. The German army conquered one European country after another. In May 1940 Holland was invaded.

Now there was no escape. Nazi soldiers guarded the train stations and the borders. If somehow a Jew did get out, there was almost no place to go. Country after country declared itself closed to Jewish refugees.

The ye

Jews in Amsterdam were forced to wear yellow stars on their clothing, so everyone would know who they were. They were not allowed in cinemas, parks, or swimming pools, or to ride in cars, trains, or even on bicycles. Dutch schools were closed to Jewish children. Anne was taken out of the Montessori School and sent to the Jewish Secondary School.

of the Dutch Jews

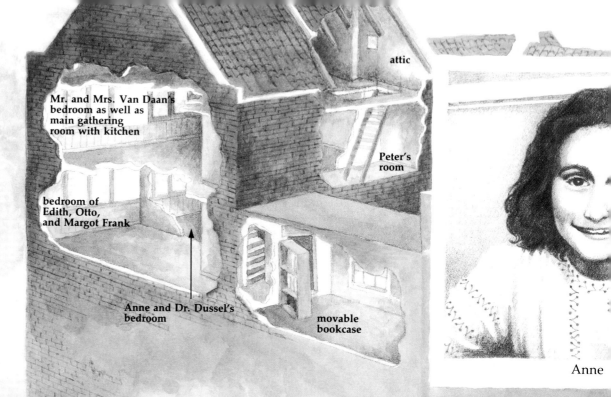

attic

Mr. and Mrs. Van Daan's bedroom as well as main gathering room with kitchen

Peter's room

bedroom of Edith, Otto, and Margot Frank

Anne and Dr. Dussel's bedroom

movable bookcase

Anne

Secret Annexe, back view

In June 1942, Anne celebrated her thirteenth birthday. She was given several gifts including a book of blank pages. Anne made it her diary and named it Kitty.

On Sunday July 5, 1942, Anne's older sister Margot was ordered to report to labour camp, where she would work in a factory.

There were other camps, too, where Jews were sent— camps where they were tortured and killed. Jews were often taken from one camp to another. The Franks knew that if Margot obeyed the Nazi order, they might never see her again.

To avoid this, the family went into hiding. Otto Frank had prepared a secret annexe or apartment in the upstairs of the building at his place of work.

263 Prinsengracht

Margot

Anne and her family needed to take clothing to the hideaway, but they couldn't be seen outside carrying suitcases. That would be a sure sign they were trying to escape. So early on Monday morning, Anne put on two vests, three pairs of pants, a dress, a skirt, and a jacket. Anne wrote in her diary that ''we put on heaps of clothes, as if we were going to the North Pole''.

Margot, Edith, Anne, and Otto Frank

Anne also carried her school bag. She could have packed it with clothes, but she didn't. She put in books, old letters, and her diary. "Memories mean more to me than dresses," Anne wrote later.

Edith Frank

Peter Van Daan

Anne Frank

Otto Frank

Dr. Dussel

There were just four rooms, a bathroom, and an attic in the secret apartment. The Franks shared it with four friends who were also hiding from the Nazis—Mr. and Mrs. Van Daan, their son Peter, and a dentist, Dr. Albert Dussel.

Mrs. Van Daan

Mr. Van Daan

Margot Frank

movable bookcase

A movable bookcase was built to hide the stairs leading to the apartment. When friends of the Franks were sure no one was watching, they brought them food, magazines, and other things. These brave Dutch people were risking their lives. They could have been sent away, too, if the Nazis discovered they were helping Jews.

During working hours, when people were in the office and warehouse below, Anne and the others had to be especially quiet. They could only whisper.

Miep Gies, friend

Anne pasted pictures of movie stars on the walls of her small room. At first she was happy there. She wrote in her diary that hiding was "like being on holiday in a very peculiar boarding house".

Soon, however, she tired of it. Day after day the food was mostly the same. After eight months Anne wrote, "We have eaten so many kidney beans and haricot beans that I can't bear the sight of them anymore." And she was with the same people all the time. They often argued.

At night Anne heard the frightening sound of large rats running about. She heard burglars robbing the warehouse below and often the sounds of sirens, gunfire, and bombs falling outside. After eighteen months in the hideaway, Anne wrote, "I am longing, so longing for everything . . . to talk, for freedom, for friends, to be alone. And I do so long . . . to cry!"

But Anne knew she was lucky. While she was hiding, other Jews were being rounded up by the Nazis.

Anne hid for more than two years. She wrote in her diary news of the war and of her growing love for Peter Van Daan who was hiding there, too.

Peter Van Daan

By the middle of 1944, Germany was losing the war. Anne and the others knew that if they could stay in hiding a while longer, they might be saved. But on Friday, August 4, 1944, their luck ran out. The Nazis found out about the hideaway and broke into it.

Anne and the others were sent in locked railway cars to Westerbork, a camp in eastern Holland. One month later they were loaded onto another train. Otto Frank knew that his family might be separated. He gave them an address in Switzerland where they could meet again after the war.

After two days and nights of travelling, the doors to the train were opened. They had been taken to Auschwitz, a Nazi death camp in Poland. Anne saw a sign above the entrance to the camp, *Arbeit Macht Frei*— "Work Will Make You Free". But that was a lie.

When prisoners arrived at Auschwitz, some were "selected" for immediate death. Others, like Anne, were saved for work. But working in the cold with little food or clothing—and suffering beatings—led to death, too.

Anne's hair was shaved off. She lost weight, but according to a woman prisoner who was also at Auschwitz and somehow survived, Anne was "still lively and sweet".

In October Anne and Margot were taken to Bergen-Belsen, a camp in Germany where there was little food and water and plenty of disease. Margot and Anne got sick with typhus. In late February or early March 1945, Margot and, later, Anne, died of disease and hunger. Anne Frank was just fifteen years old.

On May 8, 1945, the war in Europe ended. During the course of the war, six million Jews were murdered by the Nazis. One and a half million of the victims were children. Of the 120,000 Jews who had lived in Holland in 1940, just 14,000 survived. Of the eight who hid in the secret apartment in Amsterdam, only Otto Frank was left. The Nazis murdered millions of others, too, including cripples, the mentally ill, beggars, Russian prisoners of war, Romanies, homosexuals, and communists.

Otto Frank returned to Amsterdam. Someone had found Anne's diary and had given it to him. The diary was first published in 1947. Since then it has been translated into more than fifty languages. Many millions of people have read Anne's diary. They have learned from it the horrors of war, and the terrible price paid in lives and human suffering for prejudice and hatred.

Some people find it difficult to understand the enormous tragedy of the Holocaust, the organized murder of millions of people. But when they read Anne's diary, it all becomes real. Then they know one of the victims. They know Anne Frank.

NOTES FROM THE AUTHOR

The secret apartment in Amsterdam is a museum now, open to the public and run by the Anne Frank Foundation.

What later became known as *The Diary of Anne Frank* was not all kept in that first gift book of blank pages. Anne wrote in that book from June 14 until December 5, 1942, with some added notes in 1943 and 1944. A second and third volume and various loose sheets were found, too, and together they form her published diary. It was first published in Dutch under the title, *Het Achterhuis—The Annexe.*

Among the papers found in the hideaway after the Nazis arrested the Franks and the others was a list of name changes Anne planned to make if her diary were ever published. She wanted the name Van Daan to be substituted for Van Pels, and she planned to use the name Albert Dussel for Frederich Pfeffer.

For me the diary is especially poignant. Like Anne, my mother was born in Frankfurt am Main, Germany. My mother's family had also lived there for hundreds of years. My mother, along with her parents, sister, and brother, moved to Amsterdam, Holland, to escape Nazi persecution. Fortunately they left Holland in 1939, before the German invasion.

Karen Ritz used actual photographs as reference for the photographs she drew here.

The Romanies referred to in this book are commonly called Gypsies, a name many people find offensive.

David A. Adler
January 15, 1992

IMPORTANT DATES

1929 Born on June 12 in Frankfurt am Main, Germany.

1933 Moved with her family to Amsterdam, Holland.

1939 The Second World War began.

1940 On May 10 the German army invaded Holland.

1942 On June 12 Anne was given a book of blank pages for her thirteenth birthday. She made it her diary.

1942 On July 6, the Frank family went into hiding.

1944 On August 4 the Frank family was arrested along with others in their hideaway.

1944 On September 3, Anne and the others were sent to Auschwitz.

1944 In October Anne and her sister Margot were sent to Bergen-Belsen.

1945 In late February or early March Anne died in Bergen-Belsen.

1947 *The Diary of Anne Frank* was first published.

For Mom
D. A. A.

For Norine Odland
K. R.

First published 1993 by Holiday House / New York

First published in Great Britain 1994 by Pan Macmillan Children's Books
a division of Pan Macmillan Publishers Limited
Cavaye Place London SW10 9PG
and Basingstoke
and simultaneously in paperback by Piccolo

Associated companies throughout the world

ISBN 0-333-60694-9

Text copyright © David A. Adler 1993
Illustration copyright © Karen Ritz 1993

Pan Macmillan Children's Books wishes to acknowledge
The Anne Frank House, Amsterdam, The Netherlands and
The Anne Frank Fund, Basel, Switzerland, as the original source of
the Otto Frank (Anne Frank's father) photographs, many of which
were used by the artist as a basis for her work.

The right of David A. Adler to be identified as the
author of this work has been asserted by him in accordance
with the Copyright, Designs and Patents Act 1988.

1 3 5 7 9 8 6 4 2

A CIP catalogue record for this book is available from
the British Library

Printed in Hong Kong